Participant Book

CHAINED
no
MORE

A Journey Of Healing For Adult Children Of Divorce

Robyn Besemann

CHAINED NO MORE
Breaking the Chains One Link at a Time
Written and Developed by Robyn Besemann

Edited by Stephanie McIver
Cover Design by David Choates

This curriculum is not intended to be used as a replacement for therapists, counselors or other healthcare professionals. It is designed to be an additional resource to assist in the healing process. If further help is needed, please refer individuals to a psychologist or health-care professional.

For more information, contact:
Robyn Besemann
E-mail address: *robyn@robynbministries.com*
Web address: *robynbministries.com*

WestBow Press books may be ordered through booksellers or by contacting:

WestBow Press
A Division of Thomas Nelson
1663 Liberty Drive
Bloomington, IN 47403
www.westbowpress.com
1-(866) 928-1240

ISBN: 978-1-4497-5392-4 (sc)
ISBN: 978-1-4497-5391-7 (e)

Library of Congress Control Number: 2012909850

Scripture taken from the Holy Bible, New International Version®. Copyright © 1973, 1978, 1984 Biblica. Used by permission of Zondervan. All rights reserved.

Print information available on the last page.

WestBow Press rev. date: 8/29/2018

TABLE OF CONTENTS

WELCOME TO CHAINED NO MORE

Are you struggling with issues of trust, abandonment, betrayal, anger, or depression? Could it be that these issues might have begun with the separation/divorce of your parents? Could it be from other childhood trauma?

Are you finding it difficult to have a healthy, committed relationship? Do you find it hard to solve feelings of low self-worth, and do you feel as if you have to please everyone in your life?

Chained No More may be just the resource you need to help you break the chains that have been stopping you from being the best you can be!

With modern-day divorce rates at a high level, many people are opting to live together so they don't have to make the commitment of marriage. Many families have experienced multiple generations of divorce, so people are afraid to take the step of marriage. Many end up living together, which God said is not in His best plan for us.

My ministry passion has always been to help people understand who God says they are, not what anyone or any circumstances have ever told them. His heart hurts for ours, and He sees every tear.

Chained No More was developed to identify the chains of divorce, break those chains, accept God's links to us, and then make new chains, one link at a time. Then we can experience God's love, forgiveness, acceptance, and grace, allowing us to head toward a brighter future in freedom in Christ.

If by chance your parents were never married or never divorced, but you were, you can transfer many of the questions in this book to your own experiences.

My prayer is that *Chained No More* will help break the cycle of hurt and devastation in lives and, with the Lord's guidance and healing, break the chain leading to the next generation.

May God bless you and guide you as you journey through this program, and may you sense His presence in every session.

Blessings and Prayers,
Robyn Besemann
Robyn B Ministries
Writer/Developer, *Chained No More*

SAFETY AND RESPECT GUIDELINES

To make this class successful, it is important to feel safe to share thoughts, opinions, and feelings so we can heal and move toward a better future. Confidentiality is of utmost importance.

Please read and adhere to the following guidelines:

- This is a SAFETY ZONE. What is said in this class stays here. Please refrain from talking about what is said in class to others outside of the group.

- Show respect for one another by not interrupting, by accepting them and where they are in their lives, and refraining from using vulgar or offensive language.

- Everyone's opinions and answers are important.

- There are no wrong answers or feelings.

- Everyone should have an opportunity to speak and be heard.

- Cell phones should be silenced during class to minimize distraction.

THE CHAINS IN YOUR STORY

NAME _____ AGE _____

Are you: married _____ divorced _____ remarried
        widowed _____ never been married _____

Do you have kids?_____ How many? _____ Stepkids?_____ How many? _____

Are your biological parents alive? _____

Do you have stepparents? _____

Do you have brothers/sisters? _____ How many? _____

Do you have stepbrothers/stepsisters? _____ How many? _____

What five-letter word best describes you (e.g., angry, happy, corny, jaded, tired, brave)? _____

What positive talents do you have (e.g., music, sports, mechanical, writer, crafty, artistic)? _____
_____
_____

Describe God in one sentence: _____
_____
_____

Why did you decide to come to *Chained No More*? _____
_____
_____
_____
_____

LINKS IN YOUR CHAIN

(Part One)

IDENTIFYING

SESSION ONE
Links In Your Chain (Part One)
Beginning The Journey

Welcome to the first week of *Chained No More*! The most important part of session one is to begin to build trust in the group. Everyone should feel safe to share his or her feelings without fear of judgment.

 ## SESSION GOALS

- Begin to get to know one another
- Begin to build trust in leaders and group members
- Learn about the purpose of *Chained No More* and how you can benefit the most from it
- Understand the Safety and Respect Guidelines so you feel safe and valued
- Identify and acknowledge the issues that may have been caused by the divorce of your parents and other painful childhood experiences

⭐ JUST FOR YOU

We are so glad that you have decided to come to *Chained No More*. This curriculum will take you on a journey of exploring your emotions, attitudes, and actions as a possible result of the divorce of your parents.

We encourage you to dig deep, be honest, and have an open heart and mind to what the Lord may be showing you as you head toward His healing and move forward to a brighter and healthier future. This session will start you on your way by identifying the issues linked to your past.

Here we go!

May the Lord bring you into an ever deeper understanding of the love
of God and endurance that comes from Christ. 2 Thess. 3:5

Link of Truth

Divorce is the death of a marriage, and the damage goes deep into the lives of all those involved. The children of divorce pay the highest price and must live with the issues of mistrust, abandonment, betrayal, and the loss of the dream of a happy, healthy, intact family. Our goal is to help you look back, identify the issues you have carried forward into your adult life, explore and experience a journey toward God's healing, and give you the tools to move forward toward a healthier future.

🔗 LINK OF TRUTH: U.S. DIVORCE STATS

_____% of first marriages will end in divorce

_____% of second marriages will end in divorce

_____% of subsequent marriages will end in divorce

_____% of American children will witness the divorce of their parents before age 18

_____% of children will witness their parents' second divorce

_____ unmarried couples are living together in the United States. This is an 80% increase since 1980.
NOTE: There is a higher breakup rate than for married couples.

_____% of children in our country live without a father in the home

_____ are living in single-parent households

Links of Issues

What are the issues you struggle with at this time in your life? Please fill out this page to help you identify the different issues that have held you back. Mark the issues that you deal with and then put a star by the one or two that you struggle with the most. You may also add your own at the bottom of the page.

_____ **TRUST**—Unable to trust people at their word. Had breakups because of jealousy. Unable to trust men, women, authority figures, and so on.

_____ **FEAR**—Afraid of rejection. Afraid of the dark. Afraid of failure. Afraid of getting hurt. Fear seems to enter into most everything you do.

_____ **ABANDONMENT**—Afraid someone will walk away from you if you don't say or do certain things. Afraid to be alone. Difficult to form long-lasting friendships. Always feel as if you are on the outside looking in.

_____ **BETRAYAL**—Have been let down by others so you don't get involved much. Always waiting to be hurt again. Hatred of gossip. Unable to trust.

_____ **ANGER**—Cannot seem to control your anger. You can verbally or physically attack in an instant. Angry thoughts throughout the day.

_____ **CONFIDENCE**—Don't have a healthy self-image of yourself. See the flaws much more than the positives about yourself. Have difficulty with conversations or speaking in public. Afraid you will be rejected or that you are not good enough.

_____ **FORGIVENESS**—Cannot seem to forgive those who have hurt you and not sure how. Feel that if you forgive, that person is off the hook. The pain is too great to forgive.

_____ **COMMITMENT**—Afraid to make personal commitments to others because you're fearful of being hurt or rejected. Always keep a way out of a commitment possible. Don't want to get too close to others but long for a close relationship.

_____ **DEPRESSION**—Can't seem to get out of the fog. Look at the glass half empty. Nothing ever seems to work out for you. Feel as if you are drowning in a pool of gray. Want to stay in the house and pull the covers up over your head. Loss of interest in things that used to excite you.

_____ **LONELINESS**—Feel isolated and as if no one truly cares about you. Wait for someone to call but can't make the effort to call someone else. Feel as if no one understands you or what you are going through.

_____ **FAITH**—Find it difficult to trust in the Almighty God when you have been through so much. Difficult to have faith and hope that everything will be okay.

Links of Losses

We all experience a variety of losses in life. The losses are great for the children of divorce. So much is taken away; some replaced and some taken away forever. Look at the list below and mark the losses that you have experienced as a direct result of the separation/divorce of your parents. Put a star by the losses that have been the most painful for you. You may also mark losses you have generally experienced in your life.

_____ A happy, healthy family

_____ Personal identity

_____ Security

_____ Relationships with grandparents

_____ Pets

_____ Friends

_____ School/teachers

_____ Church

_____ A relationship with your dad

_____ A relationship with your mom

_____ A relationship with your brothers/sisters

_____ A healthy childhood

_____ Financial stability

_____ Trust in people

_____ Holiday/birthday traditions

_____ House and significant items from the loss of it

Childhood innocence

NOTES

LINKS IN YOUR CHAIN
(Part Two)

IDENTIFYING

SESSION TWO
Links In Your Chain (Part Two)
Taking A Trip Back

 SESSION GOALS

- Look back to the crisis and trauma of yourparents' separation/divorce and other trauma
- Explore your experience, how it affected those involved, and the emotions involved
- Look at the possible family patterns of marriage and divorce in your immediate and extended family and how they may affect you

 JUST FOR YOU

Welcome back! We hope you benefited from your first session and that you were able to make some new friends. *Chained No More* is a program that can help you see that you are definitely not the only one who has experienced the terrible pain and disappointment of their parents' divorce.

The more you put into this program, the more you will get out of it. There is no judgment here, but there *is* acceptance and understanding, led by leaders who truly care. We hope you find this a safe place to take this journey of healing.

Although we are talking about and exploring the divorce of parents, we do not wish to disrespect your parents in any way. However, we do want to face the effect their divorce had on you and then walk toward healing from the damage it caused you along with other painful experiences, as you have moved into adulthood.

> *Remember, O Lord, Your great mercy and love, for they are from of old.*
> *Remember not the sins of my youth and my rebellious ways; according to*
> *Your love, remember me, for You are good. O Lord. Psalm 25:6,7*

The Chains of Your Parents' Divorce

The divorce of parents can often begin bringing devastation and damage to children, following them all their lives. Going back and recognizing the effect your parents' divorce may have had on you can be a beginning step to a brighter future, allowing you to be free of the heavy chains from it. If your parents were not divorced, you can go to the next page to write about another trauma you experienced.

Please fill out the following questions and feel free to use the back of this page to expand on your thoughts.

Year of your parents' divorce _____ How old were you then? _____

Did you see it coming? _____

_____

How did you learn that they were separating? _____

_____

What do you remember about that conversation/revelation? _____

_____

_____

_____

How did you feel? _____

What was your reaction? _____

_____

Did someone comfort you? _____ Who? _____

How? _____

How long after that did the one parent move out? _____

Were you there when your parent moved out? _____

Was it a one-time event or was there a lot of going back and forth/moving in and out? _____

_____

With whom did you live? _____

How was that decided? _____

Were you able to see both parents? _____

Why or why not? _____

_____

If so, how often? _____

Were you able to live with your siblings? _____

_____

How long was it before your parents went to court? _____

_____

During the process, how would you describe your parents' relationship or communication? _____

_____

_____

Were you kept informed about what was going on in court? _____

_____

By who? _____

What emotions began to surface? _____

_____

Did your behavior begin to change? _____

If so, how? (For example, fighting, isolation, lower school grades, depression, and so forth) _____

_____

_____

Family Footprints

Write our thoughts about the marriage of your biological parents on the following page.

If your parent(s) remarried, do you remember the day your parent told you that he or she was going to get married to someone else? Do you remember the feelings you had? Were you happy, scared, angry, or did you just dismiss it? Most parents will date and marry again—some successfully and some unsuccessfully.

Please fill out the page below to explore only that which applies to your story. To remind you, you may transfer these questions to your own marriages, if you wish.

MOTHER
How many times has your mother been married? _____

First remarriage—year your mother married again: _____ until _____
Write your thoughts on that marriage:

Second remarriage—year your mother married again: _____ until _____
Write your thoughts on that marriage:

FATHER
How many times has your father been married? _____

First remarriage—year your father married again: _____ until _____
Write your thoughts on that marriage:

Second remarriage—year your father married again: _____ until _____
Write your thoughts on that marriage:

:

NOTES

UNDERSTANDING THE LINKS

CONNECTIONS

SESSION THREE
Understanding The Links
The Chain Of Grief

 SESSION GOALS

- Begin to look at the "Chain of Grief"
- Recognize where you think you are at this point on that chain
- Explore the denial and bargaining portion of the "Chain of Grief" and see how you may have used these in the past and may still be using them today
- Look at the subjects of betrayal and trust and how they may still be playing out in your life today

 JUST FOR YOU

Whether the divorce of your parents was last year or thirty years ago, the grief you felt or may still feel is real. Just when you think you are over it, some experience, smell, sound, or touch may bring it all back to you.

You have every right to grieve over the horrible pain you may be feeling. Divorce may be beyond painful and can affect most every area of your life: your relationships, self-worth, decision making, habits, addictions, issues of faith, and so on. The same can be said for any trauma you have experienced.

So why are we asking you to relive all of it again? Why bring it up and suffer the emotions of it again? Because, friend, it is important to see the full effect it has had on you and your future. Other benefits include finding healing in Jesus, learning the tools to have better relationships, finding higher self-worth in whom God made you to be, making better decisions, as well as dropping bad habits and addictions. Another important benefit is renewing your faith in a God who loves you no matter what. Now, isn't that worth it?

Teach me Your way, O Lord; and I will walk in Your truth;
give me an undivided heart, that I may fear You.
Psalm 86:11

Chain of Grief

The breakup of a family is reason for grief and all the emotions that are part of that. At the beginning of your parents' separation, you might have lived in denial and believed that everything would be okay. Maybe you began to bargain with your parents, yourself, or God. (For instance, *"If I get better grades, maybe my parents will be happier and won't divorce."*) Maybe you were buried by anger when you realized that there was nothing you could do about your family crisis. Depression is a large part of the grief cycle, and you may have lived with depression for quite some time; you may even still be struggling with it at times. Issues of other trauma, such as abuse of any kind, may have layers, as well.

You may have processed many emotions already, and some you may have not faced yet. Processing through the chain of grief can take a long time, and you may slip back and forth between links. Everyone deals with grief differently, so there is no "normal" way. Take your time. Study the chain below and feel free to add your own emotions on it. Please put an X beside where you are today on the grief cycle concerning the divorce of your parents, or if your parent (s) remarried and divorced again. You may also choose to address other chains from other crisis in your life, such as the death of a loved one, your own divorce, loss of a relationship, etc. You may also put an X by where you are concerning those and then label each one.

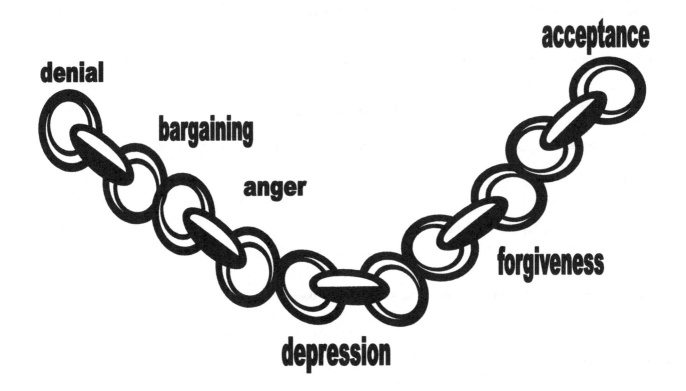

Chain of Grief: Denial and Bargaining

When your parents first said they were getting a separation/divorce, did you deny that it was happening because you hoped it wouldn't? Did you think you could bargain it away? Maybe someone close to you died or you suffered another type of loss.

DENIAL: *"There is no way this is going to happen. They will work it out."* We try to minimize the situation. *"He just can't be dead! They made a mistake."*

BARGAINING: *"Maybe if I get better grades and clean my room, they won't fight so much and won't divorce." "Maybe I could invite both of my parents out to dinner and it could rekindle their love for each other."* Bargaining can turn into manipulation. *"Maybe if I just stay quiet and comply, my spouse will stay."*

Getting stuck in denial can keep you from facing the reality of a situation. It can stop you from processing through healing from the start.

Getting stuck in bargaining can keep you unsuccessfully trying to prevent what is going to happen anyway and keep you from accepting a situation.

Trying to bargain with God is like trying to get Him down to MY expectations instead of rising to His. Do you see?

WHAT ABOUT YOU?

How much of the pain from your parents' separation/divorce have you handled with denial? (0-100%) _____

In what other areas of your life have you used denial? _____
_____

How did it change the reality of the situation? _____
_____

In what ways did you try to bargain/manipulate during your parents' divorce? _____
_____

How did it change the situation? _____
_____

Have you ever tried to bargain with God about something? _____

How did it work? _____
_____
_____

Betrayal / Trust

What does trust mean to you? _____

_____

How easy is it for you to trust people? _____

_____

How does this play out in your life? _____

_____

How does a person build trust? _____

_____

How does a person lose trust? _____

_____

Who do you feel has betrayed you in your life? List any names here, putting an X by those you believe you have truly forgiven:

_____ _____ _____

_____ _____ _____

In what relationship(s) would you like to rebuild trust? How can you begin to rebuild your trust with those people?

_____

_____

God's Idea of Trust

Trust means believing in someone or depending on them. Sometimes it means trusting them to help us out in life, especially in a time of crisis or need. *Only* the Lord is worthy of absolute trust. Because God can be trusted, His Word is also trustworthy, and we can depend on it.

All too often, however, we put our trust in other people to help us out in times of trouble, but the Bible warns us that other people can and often will disappoint and fail us. Security is never to be found ultimately in other people or in things; it can only be found in a relationship with the Lord, Who brings freedom and fullness as we trust in Him.

Looking at the diagram below, our trust in others can crack over time or be obliterated by one betrayal. We can still land on our trust in the Almighty God.

If our trust in others is broken by their own brokenness, we can still have a solid foundation of God's love and faithfulness.

 ## FROM GOD'S WORD

The Lord is good, a refuge in times of trouble. He cares for those who trust in Him. (Nah. 1:7)

Trust in the Lord with all your heart and lean not on your own understanding; in all your ways acknowledge Him and He will make your paths straight. (Prov. 3:5)

Many are the woes of the wicked, but the Lord's unfailing love surrounds the man who trusts in Him. (Ps. 32:10)

We wait in hope for the Lord; He is our help and our shield. In Him our hearts rejoice, for we trust in His holy name. May Your unfailing love rest upon us, O Lord, even as we put our hope in You. (Ps. 33:20-22)

NOTES

NOTES

POWER OF THE CHAIN

"His divine power has given us everything we need for life and godliness through our knowledge of Him who called us by His own glory and goodness, through these He has given us His very great and precious promises, so that through them, you may participate in the divine nature and escape the corruption in the world caused by evil desires" (2 Peter 1:3–4).

SESSION FOUR
Power Of The Chain
Family Patterns And Their Effects

SESSION GOALS

- Explore your family's patterns of divorce
- Look at the issues in your family, how they dealt or deal with them, and then see how you have continued or broken those patterns in your personal life
- Look at the positive/negative effects your parents have had on you
- Explore the issue of keeping secrets and lies concerning your parents' divorce and other experiences, and the effect it has on you today
- Look at what was/is your fault and what was/is not, as well as what is in your control and out of your control

JUST FOR YOU

This could be a deep session for you as you explore the effects you see from the parenting you had. You will look at family patterns in various areas and see the effects in your own life as an adult.

Children often feel that their parents' divorce was their fault. For instance, they might feel that if they had just done better in school or were more faithful in doing their chores, their parents may have not fought as much and would have stayed together. Some children are actually told they were to blame for the breakup of their family. Children also, many times, believe there was something wrong with them or it was their fault they were abused.

Take the time to dig deep and see where some of your behaviors and attitudes came from. It may just open the door to healing for you!

Turn my eyes away from worthless things; preserve my life according to Your Word. —Ps. 119:37

Family

The rate of divorce has increased over the years and many times goes from generation to generation in a family. How about yours? Who in your family tree has been divorced?

_____ PARENTS	Approx. years married _____
_____ GRANDPARENTS	Approx. years married _____
_____ GRANDPARENTS	Approx. years married _____
_____ AUNT/UNCLE	Approx. years married _____
_____ AUNT/UNCLE	Approx. years married _____
_____ SIBLING	Approx. years married _____
_____ SIBLING	Approx. years married _____
_____ CHILD	Approx. years married _____
_____ CHILD	Approx. years married _____
_____ OTHER	Approx. years married _____
_____ OTHER	Approx. years married _____

How many times has your mom been divorced? _____

How many times has your dad been divorced? _____

Name people in your life who have been married for over twenty years and never been divorced: _____

_____

_____

Why do you feel those long term marriages were so successful?

_____

_____

Living in the House: Family Patterns

To understand the links in your family chains, you must recognize the behavior patterns, acknowledge them, see the influence they had over you, and understand how they have affected your life. Once you understand the links, you can then decide what changes you want to make.

Some patterns are positive, such as encouragement, laughter, taking personal responsibility, and handling frustration in a healthy way. Some patterns are negative, such as yelling, stomping out of the room, ignoring the situation, belittling others, physical abuse, and so forth.

Please fill out the page below as you recognize some of the patterns you had in your house, including which person you had the issue with, how the family dealt with that person/issue and how it has influenced your life as an adult.

EXAMPLE:

MAKING PROMISES—Person involved: Dad
Family pattern: Never trusted his word; just "wait and see"
Personal pattern: Conscientious about keeping my word and always being on time

CONFLICT/CONFRONTATION—Person involved: _____

Family pattern: _____

Personal pattern: _____

INTEGRITY/HONESTY—Person involved: _____

Family pattern: _____

Personal pattern: _____

KEEPING HOME CLEAN—Person involved: _____

Family pattern: _____

Personal pattern: _____

DISCIPLINE—Person involved: _____

Family pattern: _____

Personal pattern: _____

HEALTHY LIFESTYLE—Person involved: _____

Family pattern: _____

Personal pattern: _____

What About Parenting?

We are all a product of our parenting, good or bad. Some of us had a healthy upbringing, while many of us lived in dysfunctional homes where stress and conflict were a normal way of life. What are some of the ways your upbringing has affected your life so far? Please fill out the section below and identify which of the parenting behaviors apply to you. Dig deep so you can get the most out of it.

NOTE: This is *not* meant to be about blaming your parents for their behaviors or their decisions in life. This is just to identify how your childhood may have affected you.

PARENTING	EFFECT ON YOU
Parents yelling at each other	
Parent leaving the family	
Giving you all you wanted	
Your sibling being "the favorite"	
Verbal abuse	
Strict religiously	
No religion/faith	
Discouraging/encouraging words	
Not being involved in your activities/sports	
Physical violence in the home	
Drug/alcohol abuse	
Being lied to	
Broken promises	
Caring grandparents	
Never good enough	

Now look at your own parenting and see the effects your parenting may have had on your own kids. Do you see a pattern?

Secrets and Lies

Many kids who live through the divorce of their parents are expected to keep secrets, be message carriers, act as spies, and lie for their parents through the battle of divorce. Please fill out the page below as you explore these issues.

Note: If this page does not apply, please fill out the next page only.

If you went to visit a parent, were you "interrogated" after the visit by your other parent? _____

If so, how did it make you feel? _____

_____

How did you deal with it? _____

_____

Did your parent(s) ask you to lie to your other parent? _____

What were some of the things you were told to lie about? _____

_____

Did you feel you had a choice? _____ How did you deal with this issue? _____

_____

Were you expected to keep secrets between your parents? _____ What kinds of secrets? _____

_____

Was it difficult for you to keep the lies and secrets straight between your parents?

_____

_____

Explain:

Do you think keeping secrets and lying for your parents has affected your life as you have grown? _____

How? _____

_____

_____

Mark the things you see in yourself, then write why you checked them. Time to get real.

_____ Tend to be able to tell believable lies

_____ Difficulty keeping things confidential

_____ Difficulty trusting the word of other people

_____ Cynical a lot of the time

_____ Confident that people are all liars

_____ Find it easy to blame others

_____ Tend to choose friends who are straight up

_____ Find yourself being very blunt sometimes

_____ Find that you almost interrogate people about things

_____ Afraid to make a commitment because you might be lied to

_____ Don't believe anything people tell you

_____ Don't feel safe enough in relationships to be honest and open

_____ Keep people at arm's length emotionally and physically

_____ Constantly searching for anyone to fill the void

_____ Find yourself prone to gossiping because of anger inside or feeling as if you have to be the "secret holder"

_____ Get defensive whenever anyone asks you too many questions

It's Not My Fault

How many times have you blamed someone else for something you were responsible for? How many times have you blamed yourself for something that was completely out of your control?

Please fill out this page to see where responsibility and blame do or do not lie in your life.

MY RESPONSIBILITY	NOT MY RESPONSIBILITY	
		The weather
		The parents I have
		The divorce of my parents
		The lifestyle of my parents
		My lifestyle choices
		My relationship with God
		My education success/failure
		My future
		My living conditions
		The price of gasoline in the United States
		Health care in America
		My use of drugs/alcohol
		My parents' use of drugs/alcohol
		My relationship with others
		Childhood abuse
		Anger reactions
		Abuse I have done to others
		Breakup of my relationship
		My parents' relationship
		My mom/dad leaving
		My siblings' choices

NOTES

NOTES

GRIP OF THE CHAIN

ANGER

SESSION FIVE
Grip Of The Chain
Recognizing Anger

SESSION GOALS

- Focus on getting a grip on your possible anger before it grips *you*
- Identify your reactions of anger as well as what sets you off
- Discuss your anger at God and how you can deal with that
- Find healthy ways to diffuse your anger

JUST FOR YOU

Anger is an emotion that can be easy to get to but very hard to get out of. It can build and build, or it can catch us off guard. You may have been raised around a lot of anger, causing you to see and feel the results of that. You may also find that you are "just like your dad/mom" when it comes to anger, and you may want to change that pattern.

Are you still mad at one or both of your parents? *Being angry isn't necessarily wrong, but what you do with it can be very wrong.*

You may also be mad at God for letting divorce abuse, or any other hurtful issues happen to your family. We will explore the issue of anger in this session. We will discuss healthy ways to deal with and express your anger.

My dear brother, take note of this; everyone should be quick to listen, slow to speak, and slow to become angry, for man's anger does NOT bring about the righteous life that God desires. —James 1:19-20

Write down some words that describe the different levels of anger.

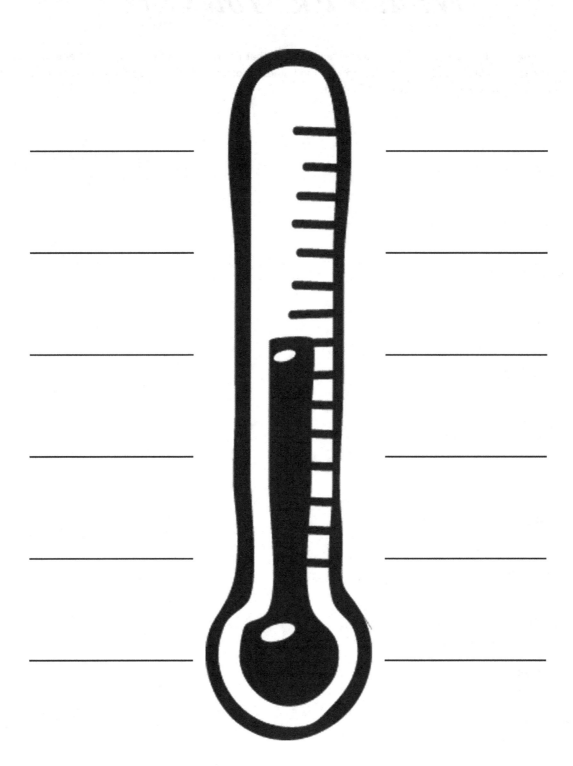

Now circle the level of anger that you may be experiencing in your life today.

What Ticks You Off?

Everyone gets angry at times, and everyone has certain buttons that people push that can make us angry. Please fill out the page below and explore what ticks you off, and why the highest scoring ones make you the angriest, because you may find some more links to your chain. (1-lowest   5-highest)

<u>Level of Anger (1-5)</u>

_____ Being lied to   _____

_____ Someone breaking a promise   _____

_____ Issues in our country   _____

_____ Injustice   _____

_____ A bad hair day   _____

_____ Being misunderstood   _____

_____ Favoritism   _____

_____ Wrongly accused   _____

_____ Someone leaving you   _____

_____ Being yelled at   _____

_____ Being disrespected   _____

_____ Being ignored   _____

_____ Other _____   _____

Link of Truth

Anger can be a tricky emotion because it can sneak up on you or sit and smolder for a long time before you feel it strongly.

One day you think you are over an offense and have forgiven the person, and all of a sudden, something triggers your anger. Maybe it is a smell or the taste of something. Maybe you see that person again and all the memories come flooding back—and you find that it still has a strong power over you.

There will always be conflict and differences of opinions. There will always be two sides to a story, and there will always be people who feel they need to win an argument.

As far as adult children of divorce are concerned, there may have been many years of built-up anger because of the breakup of the family. Pushing it aside is not the answer; making everyone else pay for it is not the answer either.

The answer is to face it head-on and look at the issues, see the painful power it has over you, seek healing, learn to forgive, and become free from the anger that has gripped you.

We can't help the first thought we have, but we sure can help the second and third and whether we dwell on them. At the first sign of anger, we have a decision as to how we are going to respond. We have the choice of whether or not to be in control.

Let's get started!

Signs of Anger

It is important to know what pushes your buttons, but it also helps to know what your first signs of anger are so you can identify them and control your anger sooner rather than later. Which of these do you experience?

_____ Gritting teeth

_____ Tightening shoulders

_____ Making fists

_____ Yelling

_____ Hitting

_____ Falling silent

_____ Turning and walking away

_____ Isolating yourself

_____ Raising your eyebrows

_____ Breathing deeper

_____ Tighten lips

_____ Blaming self

_____ Grunting or making other noises

_____ Folding arms

_____ Self-medicating (e.g., using TV, drugs, alcohol, books, food, sex)

_____ Slamming doors

_____ Throwing things

Now, consider why you have these reactions. Were they family patterns while you were growing up? More chains.

Are some of them acceptable to you? Are there some you desire to change? Are some harmful to you or others?

Managing Your Anger

It is important to recognize what negatively effects you and learn to nurture yourself. Here are some ways to release angry feelings in a healthy and safe way. Look at the list below and check the ones you have used in the past. Now look at the list again and circle the ones you would be willing to try:

- Exercise.

- Take a long, slow walk.

- Cry.

- Determine if this is something within your control or not (or needs to be).

- Talk about it with a person you can trust (a friend, teacher, pastor, counselor, family member), someone who is a good listener.

- Close your eyes, breathe deeply, and let yourself feel angry until it slowly begins to fade away.

- If you are angry, don't watch violent movies, play violent computer/video games, or listen to loud music. They may influence you, increasing the anger or causing you to act out in destructive ways.

- Take a hot bath or a cold shower, whatever "cools" you down.

- Work on any kind of puzzle or problem that needs solving. This can serve as a great distraction and keep your mind busy.

- Listen to some relaxing music.

- Sing uplifting and positive songs.

- Write a letter or write in your journal.

- Do anything that calms you down. Go to the park. Watch the sun set, gaze at the moon, sit by a lake or the ocean.

- Talk to God aloud about the issues you are angry about. Lay it all out to Him (He knows it anyway!). In doing this, you will not only be communicating with Him, but you will also be able to hear yourself and the anger you carry rather than denying it.

- The author puts it this way ... "It is important to 'put a permanent ridge in your tongue' and think before you speak." It could just save a relationship or a job!

- Learn to hold your tongue and think before you speak. Staying in control of yourself is important.

- Read the scriptures concerning anger and keeping peace in obedience to His Word.

ANGER: Three Ways to Deal with It

(Adapted from *The Big D... Divorce Thru the Eyes of a Teen - by Krista Smith*)

1. **TAKING IT OUT ON OTHERS—**This aggressive way of dealing with anger includes hitting, screaming, cussing, accusing others, putting others down, damaging property, and so on. It is destructive, tends to hurt others, and resolves little. Aggressive anger is often directed toward "safe" people, such as family members or friends.

2. **HOLDING IT IN—**You can passively bottle your feelings by not talking about them. Anger still comes out in pouting and withdrawing as the person tries to punish others, but it usually hurts the angry person the most.

3. **TALKING IT OUT—**This is the assertive way: honestly and openly telling others that you feel mad—and why. You can be animated and loud or soft and reasonable. When we talk out our anger, we move through it and don't have to stay angry too long.

Be ... quick to listen, slow to speak and slow to become angry ...
—James 1:19-20

God's Word on Anger

Anger is not wrong. If it was wrong, why would God create this emotion? How can we use this emotion effectively without hurting others?

God has a lot to say about the emotion of anger and is clear in His Word about the boundaries we should use, whether we are just a little "ticked off" or feeling rage. He wants us to control our anger, leaving revenge and justice to Him.

QUESTION: Who/what causes us to lose control of our anger?

Dr. Kimball Hodge says, "Ephesians 4:26–27 is a fantastic verse on anger. The Greek language says 'Be angry,,,.' In the NIV, it says, 'In your anger do not sin.' The 'be angry' can be productive (anger can resolve situations, producing determination or motivation). It can also become destructive when it is misdirected (for instance, bitterness turning into resentment, wrath, and rage)."

Verse 27 says, "Don't let the sun go down while you are still angry," and do not give the devil a foothold.

NOTE: This does not mean you have to stay up until 4 am hammering out every issue together before going to sleep. The original text of the Bible says to seek peace with God before the sun goes down. Sometimes conflict resolution can take several days or more to work through.

 ## FROM GOD'S WORD

A gentle answer turns away wrath, but a harsh word stirs up anger. (Prov. 15:1)

A fool gives full vent to his anger, but a wise man keeps himself under control. (Ps. 29:11)

An angry man stirs up dissension and a hot-tempered one commits many sins. A man's pride brings him low, but a man of lowly spirit gains honor. (Prov. 29:22–23)

NOTES

UNDER THE GRIP OF THE CHAIN

WHAT'S REALLY GOING ON?

SESSION SIX
Under The Grip Of The Chain
Exploring What Is Behind Anger

SESSION GOALS

- Learn what is *really* under all that anger
- Become familiar with the names of many emotions
- Identify the worries you felt because of your parents' divorce and other trauma
- Identify the emotions you are feeling and release your pain

JUST FOR YOU

During this session, we are going to look at the many emotions that could be connected in the separation or divorce of your parents or other issues in your life. It won't be easy to dig deeper into how we feel, but it is a necessary step to walk closer to healing.

Please remember that this is a safe place for you to reveal your feelings and issues. It is important not to continue to bury emotions but allow them to come to the surface in order to deal with them and experience healing.

Remember, we are all working toward the healing that comes from God, so we need to be open and honest and be willing to let His Holy Spirit do some business in our hearts. Take a deep breath and let's get started.

The Lord is a shelter for the oppressed, a refuge in time of trouble. Those who know Your name trust in You, for You, O Lord, have never abandoned anyone who searches for You. —Ps. 9:9-10

Anger Umbrella

Anger is an emotion that covers up other feelings you are also experiencing. Everyone gets angry, but with a closer look, you might find the emotions of frustration, sadness, betrayal, fear, abandonment, hurt, and so forth. It is important to recognize these feelings so you can deal with them in a healthy way. Let's try it ...

LAST TIME YOU WERE ANGRY:

Who or what: _____

Reason: _____

_____

_____

DIG DEEP

What were some other emotions you were feeling? _____

_____

_____

SITUATION #2

Who or what: _____

Reason: _____

_____

_____

Other emotions: _____

_____

_____

SITUATON #3

Who or what: _____

Reason: _____

_____

_____

Other emotions: _____

_____

_____

SITUATION #4

Who or what: _____

Reason: _____

_____

_____

Other emotions: _____

_____

_____

Worry, Worry, Worry

Stress and worry are parts of our everyday lives and can cause health problems, lack of concentration, loss of relationships and jobs, and so on. Many times, stress and worry are behind the anger that we feel.

Can you remember when you were a little kid, before your parents' divorce, and how carefree you may have been?

Now can you remember how worried and confused you were when your family split apart? Identify some of the things you worried about during that time in your life. You may also add additional things you worried about as a child. It will show you the weight that worry had on you as a kid. You may also consider the same hurts your own kids felt when you divorced.

Where would I live?

Would I see both of my parents?

Would I have to change schools?

Would we be poor?

Would my parents stop loving me too?

Was the divorce my fault?

Would I get divorced in my life?

What would the judge say about our family?

Would other kids make fun of me or ignore me?

Would I still get to see my grandparents?

What would happen during holidays/celebrations?

Who would decide where I lived?

What if my mom or dad remarried?

What would I tell my friends?

NOTES

WEIGHT OF THE CHAIN

DEPRESSION

SESSION SEVEN
Weight Of The Chain
Facing Depression

 ## SESSION GOALS

- Discuss depression—what it is and what it looks like
- Look at the different levels of depression and recognize where you are
- Discuss healthy and unhealthy ways to cope with depression

 ## JUST FOR YOU

Depression is a big part of the chain of grief. It may last for just a short time, and sometimes it can last for years. Depression is more than merely being sad. It is a lack of hope.

We pray that you will have hope when you finish *Chained No More*, and that you find your hope in Jesus Christ. Our leaders are here to encourage you as well as help you find some comfort in the feelings you have and find solutions to the struggles you are facing.

"May our Lord Jesus Christ Himself and God our Father, who loved us and by His grace gave us eternal encouragement and good hope, encourage your hearts and strengthen you in every good deed and word." —2 Thess. 2:16-17

Weight of the Chain: Depression

There are many experiences that may drop us into depression (divorce, loss of a loved one, abuse, addiction, family drama, loss of a job, or our very identity).

Depression comes in many forms and behaviors. Look at the depression chain below and check levels of depression you have experiences. Next, please check where you are today. Check as many as apply. Add more if you wish.

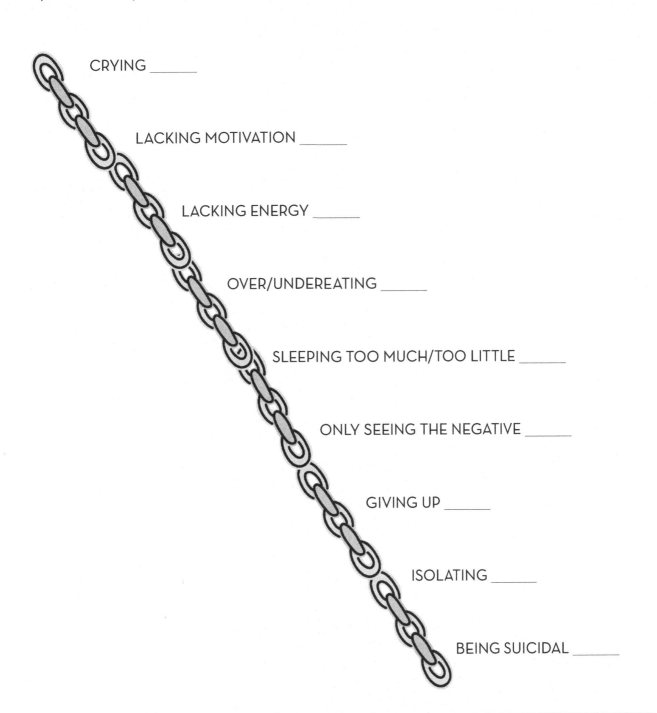

CRYING _____

LACKING MOTIVATION _____

LACKING ENERGY _____

OVER/UNDEREATING _____

SLEEPING TOO MUCH/TOO LITTLE _____

ONLY SEEING THE NEGATIVE _____

GIVING UP _____

ISOLATING _____

BEING SUICIDAL _____

Reasons for Your Depression

Please make a list of why you have experienced depression in the past and also why you may be feeling depression today.

Depression and You

You may wake up one day and feel a little sad and down, and sometimes depression can sneak up on you and make you realize that it is affecting several areas of your life. Depression can sometimes make you feel as if you are drowning and can't see a way out, or it can sometimes manifest as anger. Sound familiar?

Looking at the depression chain on page 45, determine where you are today and answer the following questions:

1. Are you feeling depressed today? _____

2. On page 45, where are you on the depression chain? _____

3. How long have you been at that level? _____

4. Do you take medication for depression? _____

5. Do you feel it is working? _____

6. Do you see a professional about this? _____ If so, how is it helpful to you? _____

_____

7. How is depression affecting your life? (Check all that you are experiencing)

_____ general feeling of sadness
_____ nothing seems fun anymore
_____ lack of concentration
_____ withdrawing/isolating from my friends
_____ want to stay in bed with the covers pulled up
_____ not sleeping well
_____ not eating well
_____ difficulty with concentration/memory
_____ difficulty making everyday decisions
_____ affecting my relationships
_____ affecting my walk with God
_____ angry feelings

"As the deer pants for streams of water, so my soul pants for You, O God, for the living God. When can I go and meet with God? My tears have been my food day and night, while men say to me all day long, 'Where is your God?' These things I remember as I pour out my soul; how I used to go with the multitude leading the procession to the house of God, with shouts of joy and thanksgiving among the festive throng. Why are you downcast, O my soul? Why so disturbed within me? Put your hope in God, for I will yet praise Him, my Savior and my God." —Ps. 42:1–5a

Depression: What Do You Do?

First of all, what are the first signs that you are headed into depression? We all get depressed at some point in our lives—from feeling slightly depressed to experiencing debilitating depression. To help you see a brighter day, what do you do when you begin to get depressed?

WHEN I FEEL BLUE:

People I talk to: _____

_____

Places I go: _____

_____

Music I listen to: _____

_____

Books I read: _____

_____

Projects I do: _____

_____

Physical activities I do: _____

_____

Movies/TV shows I watch: _____

_____

Scriptures I read: _____

_____

NOTE: Nurture yourself — It is important to nurture yourself when you realize you have a personal need or challenge. This page is a great example of this concept. As SOON as you realize you are headed into depression, begin to do the items you have written above. Don't wait until you hit bottom.

God Understands Depression

God's people suffer discouragement, depression, and even despair. There are various examples in the Bible. Some of the greatest characters in the Bible experienced depression, and on some occasions, they were so depressed that they expressed the desire to die. Many of the Psalms, including Psalm 13:1-2, 31:9-11, and 42:9-10, honestly unveil human anguish and hurt. These intense emotions, often accompanied by a sense of sadness and hopelessness, are a natural human reaction to the stresses and losses that are common to life. Many times, these feelings of depression can lead to isolation and even suicide.

God's foremost answer when we experience these emotions is to remind us that He is with us through the Holy Spirit, and that we can restore our confidence and hope through Him and in Him. At the same time, we can often receive strength and encouragement from the support, love, and concern of other believers. Reach out to someone you trust and will walk alongside of you, whether it is a family member, friend, clergy or counselor.

 FROM GOD'S WORD

Be strong and take heart, all you who hope in the Lord. (Ps. 31:24)

Turn my eyes from worthless things; preserve my life according to Your Word." (Ps. 119:37)

Humble yourselves, therefore, under God's mighty hand, that He may lift you up in due time. Cast all your anxiety on Him because He cares for you." (I Pet. 5:6-7)

NOTES

GOD'S LINK TO YOU

"*The Lord is the shelter for the oppressed, a refuge in time of trouble. Those who know Your name trust in You, for You, O Lord, have never abandoned anyone who searches for You.*"
(Psalm 9:9–10)

SESSION EIGHT
God's Link To You
Who God Is To You

 SESSION GOALS

- Define who you are aside from the past
- Discuss who God is to you and where you learned it
- Compare your earthly parents to God, the Heavenly Father, through the truth of His Word
- Write a letter to God

 JUST FOR YOU

It is our nature to let our circumstances or the opinions/expectations of others determine our self-worth instead of basing it on who God says we are. Think about it ... *We allow people who are as flawed and fickle as we are to determine our value.* How sad is that?

During this session, we will look at who we think we are, who God says we are, and recognize the lies we have based our self-worth on.

We pray that you will realize how much God truly loves you and values you just for who He made you to be.

I will praise You because I am fearfully and wonderfully made;
Your works are wonderful, I know that full well.
—Ps. 139:14

God and You

Who is God to you? Do you even believe that there *is* a God? Do you pray to Him? Do you seek His Word for wisdom and clarity in your life? Have you accepted His Son, Jesus, to be your Savior? Do you know what that means?

Take a few minutes to explore where you are with Him today and what He means to you.

How would you describe God? _____

_____

_____

What was the religious or spiritual life like in your family when you were a child? _____

_____

_____

How is your religious/spiritual life the same as it was in your original family? _____

_____

_____

How is it different? _____

_____

_____

Do you believe in Jesus Christ? Why or why not? _____

_____

_____

If you have accepted Christ, how old were you when you did? _____

Do you believe that God loves you? Do you *feel* His love for you or just *know* about it?

_____

_____

??WHO'S YOUR DADDY??

It can be difficult for people whose parents have hurt them time and time again to be able to trust them again, although many times they wish they could. Now transfer that mistrust to trying to trust our Heavenly Father. "Why should I trust a Heavenly Father I can't see when I can't trust one I can?" Sound familiar? Look at the comparisons between a human parent and the **truth** of our "Heavenly Parent":

Human parent	Heavenly Father
Broken promises	*Let us hold unswervingly to the hope we profess, for He who promised is faithful. (Heb. 10:23)*
Walked away	*I will NEVER leave you nor forsake you. (Heb. 13:5b)*
Put me down	*But You, O Lord, are a compassionate and gracious God, slow to anger, abounding in love and faithfulness. (Exod. 34:6)*
Favored my sibling(s) over me	*Here I am! I stand at the door and knock. If ANYONE hears my voice and opens the door, I will come in and eat with him and he with Me. (Rev. 3:20)*
Betrayed my other parent	*For great is His love toward us, and the FAITHFULNESS of the Lord endures forever. (Ps. 17:2)*
Was an addict of some kind	*He is the Rock, His works are perfect, and all His ways are just. A faithful God who does no wrong; upright and just is He. (Deut. 32:4)*
Punished me physically	*God disciplines us for our good, that we may share in His holiness. (Heb. 12:10)*
Did not protect me	*He is a shield for all who take refuge in Him. For who is God besides the Lord? And who is the Rock except our God? (Ps. 18:30b–31)*
Abused me in any way	*Peace I leave with you; My peace I give you. I do not give to you as the world gives. Do not let your hearts be troubled and do not be afraid." (John 14:27)*
Did not value me	*For God so loved the world that He gave His only begotten Son, that whosoever believes in him should not perish but have eternal life." John 3:16*
Lied to me	*As for God, His way is perfect; the Word of the Lord is flawless. Ps. 18:30a*
Treated me like a slave	*It is for freedom that Christ has set us free. Stand firm, then and do not let yourselves be burdened again by a yoke of slavery. (Gal. 5:1)*
Was never there for me	*"For I know the plans I have for you," declares the Lord, "plans to prosper you and not to harm you, plans to give you hope and a future. (Jer. 29:11)*
Spent little time with me	*Though my father and my mother forsake me, the Lord will receive me. (Ps. 27:10)*
Didn't really listen to me	*You will call upon Me and come and pray to Me and I will listen to You. You will seek Me and find Me when you seek Me with all your heart. (Jer. 29:12–13)*

NOTE: Look at the list again and check the ones you experienced. Now read the verses beside them again. Speak His Truth and know Your Heavenly Father treasures you.

God's Care for You

Many of us have grown up not feeling valued. We didn't have that encouragement and support that we longed for so much. You may have felt neglected and as if nobody cared whether you lived or died.

Well, friend, God cares. He created you with gifts and talents, and He has a perfect plan for you. He values you and loves you more than you can ever imagine. Look at what His Word says about you.

 FROM GOD'S WORD
(Note author's emphasized words)

*O Lord, You have searched me and **You know me**. You know when I sit*
and when I rise; You perceive my thoughts from afar. You discern my going
*out and my lying down; You are familiar with **all** my ways.*

*Before a word is on my tongue, **You know it completely**, O Lord.*

*You hem me in—behind and before; **You have laid Your hand upon me**.*
Such knowledge is too wonderful for me; too lofty for me to attain.

Where can I go from Your Spirit? Where can I flee from Your presence? If I go up to the
*heavens, **You are there**; if I make my bed in the depths, **You are there**. If I rise on the wings*
*of the dawn; if I settle on the far side of the sea, even there **Your Hand will hold me fast**.*

You created my inmost being; You knitted me together in my mother's womb. I praise You
*because I am fearfully and wonderfully made; **Your works are wonderful**; I know that*
full well. My frame was not hidden from You when I was made in the secret place. When
I was woven together in the depths of the earth, Your eyes saw my unformed body.

All the days ordained for me were written in Your book before one of them came to be.

Search me, O God, and know my heart; test me and know my anxious thoughts.
See if there is any offensive way in me and lead me in the way everlasting.

(Portions of Psalm 139)

THIS is the truth of how much God loves, accepts, and values you. Let this Truth begin to replace all the negative messages and lies you have carried with you throughout your life.

NOTES

LETTING GO OF THE CHAIN

FORGIVENESS

SESSION NINE
Letting Go Of The Chain
Receiving And Giving Forgiveness

 **SESSION GOALS**

- Explore and define what forgiveness is and what it isn't
- Discuss the depth of God's forgiveness for you
- Look at areas of your life where unforgiveness has chained you down
- Break the chain of unforgiveness in your life
- Experience God's grace and be able to give grace to others

 JUST FOR YOU

Forgiveness can be difficult. We have all been hurt and let down throughout our lives; some people are easier to forgive than others are. Sometimes the hurt is too great and we continue to live in bitterness and unforgiveness.

Forgiveness is often about what you have lost—maybe wrong decisions by people we love or even for our own mistakes; maybe for the way things turned out.

The first step toward forgiveness is to be willing to try to forgive. Ask the Lord to help you and open your eyes to His forgiveness and yours.

Bear with each other and forgive whatever grievances you may have
against one another. Forgive as the Lord forgave you.
—Colossians 3:13

How do You Spell
F-O-R-G-I-V-E-N-E-S-S?

Please write a word or phrase that reflects your thoughts/beliefs about forgiveness, with each letter of the word "forgiveness."

F

O

R

G

I

V

E

N

E

S

S

Forgiveness: Right or Wrong?

Please look at the following quotes and indicate whether you agree or disagree.

AGREE	DISAGREE	QUOTE
		"Strength of character means the ability to overcome resentment against others, to hide hurt feelings and to forgive quickly."
		"One of the secrets to a long and fruitful life is to forgive everybody everything before you go to bed."
		"To forgive is to set a prisoner free and discover that the prisoner was *you!*"
		"Two persons cannot be friends for long if they cannot forgive each other's little failings."
		"When a deep injury is done to us, we never recover until we forgive."
		"You must have been given forgiveness to give forgiveness to someone else."
		"He who is devoid of the power to forgive is devoid of the power to fully love."

Is it easy for you to forgive? Why or why not? _____

_____

What has been the most challenging thing you've had to forgive someone for? _____

_____

_____

Forgiveness: Fact or Fiction?

Put a "T" or "F" for each statement:

_____ Forgiving someone means that you will no longer get angry or have any more negative feelings.

_____ If you forgive, you have to put it all behind you and leave it in the past, becoming friends with the person who hurt you.

_____ You do not have to forgive an immoral person.

_____ You may want to forgive someone, but you may not be ready on the inside.

_____ Forgiving is necessary in the healing process, and you will not be able to completely heal until you do so.

_____ You cannot forgive until the offender asks for forgiveness or shows that he or she is sorry.

_____ When you forgive others, you believe and accept that God has forgiven you.

_____ If you forgive someone, you have to forget what that person has done.

_____ Forgiveness depends on getting a guarantee that someone won't do the same wrong thing again.

_____ Forgiveness is unconditional.

_____ Forgiveness excuses the other person's sin or wrongdoing.

(Adapted from *The Big D...Divorce Thru the Eyes of a Teen*, by Krista Smith)

God's Forgiveness To You

If we confess our sins, He is faithful and just and will forgive us
our sins and purify us from all unrighteousness.
(1 John 1:9)

Working through forgiveness is one of the most difficult things you may have to do in your journey of healing. In order for us to truly forgive someone, we need to understand and experience God's forgiveness for us. Do you believe that God's Word is Truth? _____ All of it? _____

The Bible says that God sent His only Son, Jesus, to be cruelly beaten and nailed to a cross long ago so that you would not have to pay the penalty of death for the sins you commit. What is your response to this?

_____

_____

Have you accepted God's forgiveness for you from *all* your sins—past, present, and future? _____

_____

Do you believe He won't forgive these sins? _____ If so, why? _____

_____

Looking back on your life so far, and looking at all the sins you have committed and the people you have hurt, do you believe that God has forgiven you and keeps no record of wrong?

_____

_____

What sins do you believe you have done that you fear God cannot or will not forgive? _____

_____

_____

For all have sinned and fall short of the glory of God and are justified freely
by His grace through the redemption that came by Christ Jesus.
(Romans 3:23-23)

God's Truths on Forgiveness

It is difficult for humans to truly understand God's idea of forgiveness. We would rather write somebody off if that person has severely hurt us, right? After all, why set ourselves up for more hurt? That person doesn't deserve to be forgiven. Wait a minute! That is not God's idea of forgiveness. He is extremely specific as to how He would have us deal with the issue of forgiveness.

Because of God's compassion, love, grace, and mercy, He offers pardon for our sins by putting them out of sight, out of reach, out of mind, and out of existence. Christ's shedding of His blood on the cross is the ultimate sacrifice, and that loving act took all our sins, all the selfishness, the hatred, the deceit, and the pride and nailed them to the cross so that those who believe might be declared innocent and free from sin's controlling power. He asks us to forgive others as well, although it doesn't mean we need to make the ultimate sacrifice as He did. How can we refuse?

Hopefully, you have learned what forgiveness is and is not through this session. Now let's look a little deeper.

 FROM GOD'S WORD

*If You, O Lord, kept a record of sins, O Lord, who could stand? But with
You, there is forgiveness; therefore You are feared. (Ps. 130:3-4)*

*For if you forgive men when they sin against you, your Heavenly Father will also forgive you,
but if you do not forgive men their sins, your Father will not forgive you. (Matt. 6:14-15)*

NOTE: What the original text of the Bible says, is that if we don't forgive others, we will be out of fellowship with God. We will not lose our salvation.

*Bear with each other and forgive whatever grievances you may have
against one another. Forgive as the Lord forgave you. (Col. 3:13)*

Sinner's Prayer

I know I am a sinner and have done many things that do not please You.
I need Your forgiveness today.

I believe that Jesus Christ is Your Son, and that You sent Him to be brutally beaten and nailed to a cross to pay the penalty of my sins. Thank You for loving me that much.

I don't want to live in sinful ways anymore, so I am inviting Jesus Christ to come into my heart and become my own personal Savior, to cleanse me from all the sins I have committed.

I need Your help to follow You and live for Jesus Christ the rest of my life.

Growing In God

- Talk to God every day
- Read His Word
  (Begin in the book of John)
- Find a church that teaches God's Word and plug in
- Share your new faith in God with others

Lord, Please Forgive Me

Please write down the things you feel you need God to forgive you for.

I Need to truly forgive

Please write down the people you feel you need to try and forgive and for what.

Things I need to forgive Pis place this at the myself for:

Please write down the things you need to forgive yourself for so you can be free of shame .

NOTES

BREAKING THE CHAIN

If you hold to My teaching, you are really My disciples.
Then you will know the truth and the truth will set you free!
(John 8:31–32)

SESSION TEN
Breaking The Chain
Discovering The REAL You

SESSION GOALS

- Recognize the positive things about you
- Define who God wants you to be
- Look at some of the positive things that may have come from the divorce of your parents and other experiences
- Discover your spiritual gifts
- Discover what God's Word says about His children

JUST FOR YOU

We have looked back on our lives and seen what has damaged us, defined us, and affected us. Maybe we say, "Well, I was abused," or "My parent was never there for me," or "I was always told I was stupid."

These chains have held you back and kept you in their grip. These chains have kept you down and may have affected every area of your life, in personal relationships, ability to commit, lack of integrity, unable to trust, and so on.

During this session, we will look at the area of acceptance: acceptance of who God made you to be, aside from your past; acceptance of the facts of your past; and acceptance of the unconditional love of God. Acceptance is the last link of the grief chain and an important one for you to be able to move forward as you "break the chains."

> *The Lord is faithful to all His promises and loving toward all He has made. The Lord upholds all those who fall and lifts up all who are bowed down. The Lord is near to all who call on Him, to all who call on Him in truth; He hears their cry and saves them.* —Ps. 145:14, 17-19

Freedom To Be Me

We often get buried by circumstances or others' expectations of us, and we can lose ourselves in the process. We can forget who we truly are and the kind of person we want to be.

Take some time to look at who *you* are: your strengths, weaknesses, likes, dislikes, your idea of fun, your goals, and so forth. Have fun with this!

The best thing about me is _____

_____

What I would like to improve about myself is _____

_____

What I like to do to have fun is _____

_____

What I like most about my looks is _____

_____

Do I make a good friend? _____ Why or why not? _____

_____

My bucket list includes:

_____

Not So Bad

It is important to see the positive things that may have come from even bad situations. As you travel the road to healing, you will be surprised at how many good things have happened in your life as a result of damage you suffered as a kid. Please list them below.

Things I learned about myself:

1.

2.

3.

4.

5.

New people/relationships in my life:

1.

2.

3.

4.

5.

Positive changes in me:

1.

2.

3.

4.

5.

Other good things that have happened:

1.

2.

3.

4.

5.

(Adapted from *The Big D... Divorce Thru the Eyes of a Teen*, by Krista Smith)

++ *Pluses & Minuses* --

It is good to realize that not all the changes we resist turn out negatively. Take some time and list some pluses and minuses that you have experienced because of your parents' divorce or other experiences. (Example: MINUS – had to do a lot of extra chores PLUS – Became a much more responsible person)

Pluses	Minuses

(Adapted from *The Big D... Divorce Thru the Eyes of a Teen*, by Krista Smith)

Spiritual Gifts

When someone gives you a wrapped gift, do you just let it lie on the table so you can look at it, or do you open it to see what is inside? We would all open it, right?

God has given you spiritual gifts that He wants you to open and use for His glory throughout your life. Check out this scripture:

Just as each of us has one body with many members, and these members do not all have the same function, so in Christ we who are many form one body, and each member belongs to all the others. We have different gifts, according to the grace given us. If a man's gift is prophesying, let him use it in proportion to his faith. If it is serving, let him serve; if it is teaching, let him teach, if it is encouraging, let him encourage, if it is contributing to the needs of others, let him give generously; if it is leadership, let him govern diligently, if it is showing mercy, let him do it cheerfully. (Rom. 12:4-8) There is also a list of "lesser gifts" in 1 Corinthians 12.

Look at the list of spiritual gifts below and mark the one(s) that could be yours.

_____ HOSPITALITY—able to make people feel comfortable and welcome

_____ HELP—gives practical service

_____ LEADERSHIP—gives leadership and direction

_____ ADMINISTRATION—works behind the scenes to keep things in order

_____ COMPASSION/MERCY—shares a person's pain and struggles to provide support

_____ ENCOURAGEMENT—uses kind, encouraging words and actions freely

_____ SHOPPING (Just kidding!)

_____ DISCERNMENT—able to discern between right and wrong based on the Bible

_____ TEACHING—researches and teaches the Bible

_____ EXHORTATION—Encourages personal progress with honesty and openness

_____ GIVING—shares practical and material assistance

Which spiritual gifts do you presently use in serving the Lord? _____

_____

What gifts or abilities besides those mentioned here, do you see in yourself that God could use?

_____

_____

Identity Theft ... Who Am I Really?!

Many of us have defined ourselves by our circumstances, by who someone else told us we should be, or what society has told us. *Your self-image should come from who GOD says you are*, not from any human expectations. Explore the following verses and see how God designed you and values you. Be blessed!

John 1:12	I AM accepted ... I AM God's child
John 15:15	As a disciple, I am a FRIEND of Jesus Christ
Rom. 5:1	I have been JUSTIFIED
1 Cor. 6:17	I am united with the Lord, and I am ONE WITH Him in Spirit
1 Cor. 6:19-20	I have been bought with a price and I BELONG to God
1 Cor.12:27	I am a member of Christ's body
Eph. 1:3-8	I have been CHOSEN by God and ADOPTED as His child
Col. 1:13-14	I have been redeemed and forgiven of ALL my sins
Col. 2:9-10	I am COMPLETE in Christ
Heb. 4:14-16	I have DIRECT ACCESS to the throne of grace through Jesus Christ
Rom. 8:1-2	I am SECURE/I am FREE FROM CONDEMNATION
Rom. 8:28	I am ASSURED that God works for my good in ALL circumstances
Rom. 8:31-39	I am FREE from ANY condemnation brought against me, and I CANNOT be separated from the love of God
2 Cor. 1:21-22	I have been ESTABLISHED, ANOINTED, AND SEALED by God
Col. 3:1-4	I am hidden with Christ in God
Phil. 1:6	I am CONFIDENT that God WILL complete the good work He started in me
Phil. 3:20	I am a citizen of Heaven
2 Tim. 1:7	I have NOT been given a spirit of fear, but of POWER, LOVE, and a SOUND MIND
1 John 5:18	I am born of God, and the evil one CANNOT touch me
John 15:5	I am SIGNIFICANT/I am a branch of Jesus Christ, the True Vine and channel of His life
John 15:16	I have been CHOSEN AND APPOINTED to bear fruit
1 Cor. 3:16	I AM God's temple
2 Cor. 5:17-21	I am a minister of reconciliation for God
Eph. 2:6	I am seated WITH Jesus Christ in the heavenly realm
Eph. 2:10	I AM God's workmanship
Eph. 3:12	I may approach God with FREEDOM AND CONFIDENCE
Phil. 4:13	I CAN do ALL things through Christ, Who strengthens me

(Adapted from *Victory over the Darkness*, by Dr. Neil Anderson)

NOTES

LOVE LINKS
LOVE & RELATIONSHIPS

LOVE...bears all things, believes all things, hopes all things, endures all things. Love NEVER fails.
1 Corinthians 1:13

SESSION ELEVEN
Love Links
Love And Relationships

 SESSION GOALS

- Explore your thoughts and attitudes about a love relationship
- Learn about trust and respect in a healthy marriage
- Reflect on your family patterns and beliefs about vows and commitment
- Learn healthier ways to deal with conflict and confrontations
- Explore what God's Word says about love

 JUST FOR YOU

Your ideas about love and marriage have no doubt been influenced mostly by your parents' relationship. You may have seen both good and bad times and possibly the failure of their marriage.

This may have left you with a fear of commitment or the hope that your marriage will be successful. You may find it difficult to trust or be afraid they will abandon you, so why set yourself up for more hurt?

There are tools and lessons to be learned in this session to help set you up for success in marriage—a marriage based on God's principles of love and marriage. These tools can also help with other relationships in your life.

> *Love is patient, love is kind and is not jealous; love does not brag and is not arrogant, does*
> *not act unbecoming; it does not seek its own, is not provoked, does not take into account*
> *a wrong suffered. It does not rejoice in unrighteousness, but rejoices with the truth.*
> *— 1 Corinthians 13:4-6*

All You Need Is Love, Right?

We were made for relationships, romantic or not. You may have seen great long-term marriages in addition to seeing your parents' and others' marriages break up, so you may be confused as to what love and marriage are really all about—and why the Lord created them.

Please explore your thoughts, ideas and your understanding about what true love is all about on the page below.

Describe in one sentence what *love* is: _____

_____

_____

Describe in one sentence what *marriage* is: _____

_____

_____

What are two of the most important elements of a healthy marriage?

1. _____

2. _____

What is your understanding of what vows mean in a wedding ceremony (for example, for better or worse, richer or poorer, sickness or health, forsaking all others as long as we both shall live)? _____

_____

_____

_____

Is it easy for you to tell others you love them? _____

Why or why not? _____

_____

Because of your parents' divorce or other influences, what are some of the fears (e.g., mistrust, insecurity, infidelity, fear of abandonment, fear of failure, and so forth) you have about being married?

_____

_____

_____

Do you believe that love truly can last forever and that you can have a healthy marriage? _____

Why or why not? _____

_____

_____

_____

What do you think it means to "live as one" in marriage? _____

_____

_____

_____

_____

_____

Vows, Promises, and Commitment

Do you feel as if you let people down a lot? Do friends, family, and others get frustrated when you promise something and can't deliver? Do you find that you would rather walk away than make a strong commitment to a relationship?

Most children of divorce struggle with all these issues. After all, what did their parents' wedding vows mean, anyway? What is the big deal with commitment?

Please answer the questions below to explore these subjects and explain how you think your parents' divorce or other experiences have affected certain areas of your life. Please be specific.

When asked to make a commitment, what stops you? _____

_____

_____

When did others, besides your parents, break a commitment, promise, or vow to you? Write about as many as you want to.

_____

_____

How do you think these have affected you? _____

_____

_____

Are you usually late for things? _____ If so, think deeply and explain why you think that is: _____

_____

_____

How loyal of a person are you? What challenges do you face in being loyal?

_____

_____

_____

Explain what you believe integrity means: _____

_____

_____

Do you believe you are a person of integrity? _____

Would friends say you are? _____

Would your employer say you are? _____

Would your family say you are? _____

Would your children and/or grandchildren say you are? _____

Would God say you are? _____

What is a vow/promise you have kept in your life—and to whom? _____

_____

What is a vow/promise you have broken in your life—and to whom? _____

_____

When a man makes a vow to the Lord or takes an oath to obligate himself by a
pledge, he must not break his word but must do everything he said.
—Num. 30:2

What steps do you need to take to become more of a trustworthy person? _____

_____

_____

Conflict, Tensions, And Confrontation

There are many ways to face conflict; some are effective for resolving the issues, and some are not. Below is a list concerning what kind of example you had as a child growing up as well as some tools to help.

1. The general way to handle conflict in our home was:

_____ Yelling, screaming, cussing

_____ Hitting, slapping, and so forth

_____ Ignoring the situation/other person

_____ Sitting down and talking it out

_____ Talking to someone else about it instead of the person you had the conflict with

_____ Usually a lecture by a parent

_____ Usually grounded

_____ Other _____

_____

Some families are good at conflict resolution, and some are not. It depends on the communication skills in the family, whether there are addictions involved, the age of the children, and the level of good parenting skills, among other things.

This is an important area of family patterns and shows how they are passed on from generation to generation. If your parents had parents who yelled, screamed, and cussed, chances are they did the same thing in your home. If they had parents who communicated well and were willing to work out resolutions, then chances are you had that type of home growing up.

Once a pattern has been set, it can be very difficult to break that pattern. This may result in you not being excited to be a parent, whether now or in the future. You may not want your kids to grow up with the same "stuff" you did. Right?

We are here to tell you that you can certainly break patterns of verbal or physical abuse in your family if you are willing to do the work.

Here are some suggested steps to improve effective conflict resolution.

STEP ONE—Realize that there will always be differences of opinion. There are always two sides to a conflict. Each person has a right to an opinion, and it is important to look at what is behind behavior.

Note: It is important to take time to pray about and believe a peaceful and helpful resolution is possible with God's guidance.

Note: If you are so upset that you can't talk without angrily hurting the other person or damaging your relationship, you can take a step back and return later to discuss the issue when both of you have calmed down. During the time out, take deep breaths and ask God to help you come to a positive resolution.

STEP TWO—Make up your mind that you are working for a positive resolution—not to control or get your way or to prove that you are right. Do what you can to avoid a competition of wills. Have a strong resolve, but a humble spirit.

STEP THREE—Resolve in your mind that you are going to exercise patience and kindness; that the louder the other person gets, the quieter you will become and that you will not fuel the conflict. You are an adult and will control yourself. Someone has to take the high road for the sake of the relationship. Let it be you.

STEP FOUR—Learn to listen and *truly hear* what the other is trying to say. Don't think about what you are going to say next; listen *fully* to the other person and don't interrupt. Keep a check on your facial expressions as well.

STEP FIVE—When you speak, keep your voice calm but firm. Stay away from using "always" or "never." (For example: "You *always* forget to lock the door" or "You *never* do anything around here.") Such statements are not true and only put the other person on the defensive. If the other person interrupts you, stop talking and remind them that you didn't interrupt when they were speaking,, stating that you would like to finish. Let them know that you are interested in what they have to say when you finish sharing your thoughts.

STEP SIX—When both of you have given your opinions and thoughts and concerns, it is time to figure out how to resolve the conflict. After hearing each other, can you see what would be the best solution, remembering that this is not about getting your way or being in control but about resolving a conflict peacefully and keeping a strong, loving relationship in the process?

STEP SEVEN— If you need to, write down what each of you say you will do to make the necessary adjustments, ask for forgiveness, forgive each other, and if both feel comfortable, hug and make up. If possible and both agree, close the confrontation in prayer and ask the Lord to heal hurt feelings and restore your relationship.

Note: This type of process will no doubt take a longer amount of time, but the result should be a lot better than just flying off the handle and hurting one another.

Do not repay anyone evil for evil. Be careful to do what is right in the eyes of everybody. If it is possible, as far as it depends on you, live at peace with everyone [including your spouse and children].
—Rom. 12:17-18

Chained No More

Trust and Respect

Love can mean many things to many people ... It can mean a romantic dinner, caring for each other when sick, a night of passion, or just staring at the sunset together. What does the word *love* mean to *you*?

The basis for love, I believe, is trust and respect, and love becomes the result of that. If you don't have both of these elements in your love relationship, it can become more of an obligation, an existence.

TELL THE TRUTH: This is one of the most important elements to a healthy relationship. When someone lies to you or is unfaithful to you, from that moment on, your trust is lessened. What do you know you can believe? If you lied once, you can lie again, and then trust is broken. God's Word is strong about honesty and integrity. We are not children anymore, trying to get away with things; we are adults. We appreciate people being truthful with us, and we should do the same. How can I believe you are committed to me and love me if I can't trust you with simple truth?

RESPECT EACH OTHER'S PRIVACY: We do not own each other and should never treat the other person as a possession. Both should be able to have their privacy about their pasts, personal habits, and things they enjoy away from you. Now, if there is something the other person is doing that is hurting the marriage (pornography, an affair, or other hurtful actions past or present), value your relationship enough to take the time to discuss it calmly and try to resolve it together.

UNDERSTAND: We don't always know what is behind what someone tells us, do we? Try to understand why the other person is hurting and find out the "whys behind the whats". Figure out why they do certain things or have certain issues, by observing and then asking in a nonthreatening way. Both people have the right to think and do what they want to, within reason. You may never completely understand, but love each other enough to try.

SERVE EACH OTHER: God commands us to serve one another, which does not mean that one becomes a servant, so to speak. Serving one another means trying to think ahead about what the other person may need and how you can support them. This does not mean the other person is helpless; it is just another form of loving one another. This does not include keeping score about who is doing more or who cleaned it the last time. There is no room for this type of competition in marriage! Serve with love and care and full commitment to your marriage.

TRACK RECORD: It is important to know the track record of the other person. Are they a person of integrity, kindness, strong character, monogamous, honest, and so forth? If you doubt their intentions, have they given you a reason for that, or were you hurt by someone else in that area? Don't let this person pay for another person's issue. If there are issues that are difficult to get over and you see a pattern that is hurting your relationship, suggest going to a counselor or pastor. It's worth it.

REMOVE DISRESPECT OF ANY KIND: The words we use can hurt someone deeply, so avoid all putdowns, cussing, and calling each other bad names in your marriage. The Bible is full of scriptures telling us how we should treat each other. Respect each other's privacy, differences of ideas, and ways of doing things—and definitely don't disrespect the other's parenting, especially in front of your children. Never disrespect your spouse in front of others, even in jest. It only makes you look bad, and it is hurtful to your spouse and damaging to your marriage.

ETCH THE WORD OF GOD ON YOUR RELATIONSHIP: Make time in God's Word one of your priorities as a couple. Attend church together and get involved with people who are in healthy relationships so you can encourage one another in your marriage commitments. Make the time to pray for one another and with each other. Bring big decisions before the Lord together and ask for His guidance as a couple. Play worship music in your home and car and attend good concerts; there are many different styles for all tastes. Enjoy your walk with the Lord together, and keep encouraging one another in their spiritual walk.

STAND UP FOR EACH OTHER: Make sure you always have the other's back. No matter what the conflict, stand up for each other in front of others and question/confront behind closed doors. Assume your spouse is in the right unless you find out otherwise. Never let your spouse feel as if they are alone, with no one to walk alongside and defend them.

PUT COMPETITION ASIDE: Nothing can hurt a marriage more or quicker than arguments and competition. If you have to win, then you are both losers. Consider that you are trying to win an argument and want to prove that you are right. You are purposely working to prove that your spouse is wrong, and therefore you both lose. Love is not about that. It is about working together, encouraging one another in love. Next time, learn to listen and try to work together for understanding and a compromise, even if it means you agree to disagree. Now kiss and make up!

ENCOURAGE ONE ANOTHER: You may have seen your parents encourage each other, and you may have been witness to a lot of shouting and violence. Obviously, that is not the way to treat someone you said marriage vows to, right? You know how it feels to be encouraged, so give a lot of it to the one you love. Look for the things that are positive about them and let them know you appreciate them. If they are headed toward a better job, school, or another accomplishment, encourage them and help them achieve their goals. When they reach a big goal, celebrate with them and let them know how proud you are of them. When they fall, lift them up with your words and actions.

COUPLE TIME: Our world is fast-paced, and many times couples are like ships passing in the night. Intimacy fits in the schedule rarely and can become unfulfilling. Make efforts to end the evenings alone, giving you time to talk and cuddle before going to bed. Turn the TV/computer/cell phone off, take a walk, or sit on the couch and reconnect. Once a year, at least, plan a weekend away to have some time alone to enjoy each other with no distractions. Meet for lunch once a week, if possible, to connect during the week. Meet in a park, a restaurant, a mall food court ... It doesn't matter. Have fun dating again. Note: Don't assume there will be intimacy when there is conflict. Work on the conflict first, so you are both free to give and receive love.

TAKE TIME TO REALLY LISTEN: There is so much noise around us, so many distractions, and so little time to communicate face-to-face. When your spouse is sharing something, face them, stop what you are doing, and listen without thinking about what you are going to say when they takes a breath! Hear what is behind the hurt if they are sharing something that is burdening them. You don't always need to give advice; in fact, only give it if they ask. Try it. Sometimes people just need to vent and don't need you to "fix" them. Just walk beside them in love.

Extra Hints To Keep The Peace

HINT #1—Keep the main thing the main thing. When you are discussing an issue, *do not* bring up other issues from the past. If you haven't resolved a past issue, try to find another time to do that. Don't keep score by bringing up past offenses.

HINT #2—Remember that you made a *covenant*, not merely a paper contract, with your spouse at the wedding. You also made a covenant to God on that day.

HINT #3—If you and your spouse cannot resolve issues, be willing to get some guidance from a mediator, pastor, marriage counselor, or therapist. If your spouse refuses to go, be willing to go alone. Value your spouse and your marriage enough to do the work to make it work.

HINT #4—If there is a conflict, ask yourself if it is worth the relationship. Pick your battles, compromise when you can, and always be willing to apologize and genuinely ask for forgiveness if you have offended your spouse. Give grace unconditionally.

HINT #5—Pray daily for your marriage and your spouse. Then ask God to help you be the spouse He designed you to be.

Love And Gods' Word

Please look at the following scriptures and write how you think each one can apply to marriage.

Be completely humble and gentle; be patient, bearing with one another in love. (Eph. 4:2)	
Speaking the truth in love, we will in all things grow up into Him who is the Head, that is Christ. (Eph. 4:15)	
Be imitators of God, therefore, as dearly loved children, and live a life of love, just as Christ loved us. (Eph. 5:1–2)	
Serve one another in love. (Gal. 5:13)	
Whatever you do, work at it with all your heart, as working for the Lord, not for men … (Col. 3:23)	
Bear with each other and forgive whatever grievances you may have against one another. (Col. 3:13)	
A gentle answer turns away wrath, but a harsh word stirs up anger (Prov. 15:1).	
Pride goes before destruction, a haughty spirit before a fall. (Prov. 16:18)	

NOTES

NOTES

MAKING A NEW CHAIN
(Part One)

...ONE LINK AT A TIME

SESSION TWELVE
Making A New Chain (Part One)
Changing Old Patterns

SESSION GOALS

- Realize your old patterns of thoughts and behavior
- Examine who you are and who you want to become
- Reflect on the influences you have in your life and how they may be affecting you
- Allow yourself to look at your dreams for the future and find a way to achieve them

JUST FOR YOU

Here in session 12, we will look at who we have become throughout our lives to this point, and what we need to see for positive changes. No matter how old we are, there is always room for changes and improvements. This doesn't mean we can never be content, but it does mean that we should continually strive to become more like Christ and live life to the fullest, using the gifts and talents He has given to us for His glory.

We seem to want to compare ourselves to other flawed human beings, whether it is how we look, how much we have materially, and where or *if* we fit in. The question is, are we pleasing to the Lord and living up to His plan for us? *That's* the best life we could ever live!

Do not conform any longer to the patterns of this world, but be transformed
by the renewing of your mind. Then you will be able to test and approve what
God's will is ... His good, pleasing and perfect will. (Rom. 12:2)

What's On Your Mind?

Our society is full of distractions through the media, television, magazines, computer screens, music, and movies. Our minds can be overloaded with things that cloud what God has in mind for us. Using this page, explore what is on your mind.

Indicate the activities and influences you have in your life and how they may be affecting your mind.

Favorite TV shows _____
Positive influence _____
Possible negative influence _____

Movies watched _____
Positive influence _____
Possible negative influence _____

Magazines you read _____
Positive influence _____
Possible negative influence _____

Music you listen to _____
Positive influence _____
Possible negative influence _____

Computer websites _____
Positive influence _____
Possible negative influence _____

Books you read _____
Positive influence _____
Possible negative influence _____

Friends you hang out with _____
Positive influence _____
Possible negative influence _____

Free-time activities _____
Positive influence _____
Possible negative influence _____

*Whatever is **noble**, whatever is **right**, whatever is **pure**, whatever is **lovely**, whatever is **admirable** ...*
*If anything is **excellent** or **praiseworthy**, **think on these things**. —Phil. 4:8*

Looking In The Mirror

*Anyone who listens to the Word but does not do what it says is like a man
who looks at his face in a mirror and, after looking at himself, goes away
and immediately forgets what he looks like. (James 1:22-24)*

*Now we see but a poor reflection as in a mirror; then [when we get
to heaven]) we shall see God face to face. (1 Cor. 13:12)*

*We, who with unveiled faces all reflect the Lord's glory, are being transformed into His likeness
with ever-increasing glory, which comes from the Lord Who is the Spirit. (2 Cor. 3:18)*

What do you see in the mirror? Look deeper. What do you see that you like (confidence, joy, intelligence, purpose, etc.)?

What do you see that you don't like (fear, bitterness, low self-worth, failure)?

What do you *want* to see in the mirror?

What are you willing to do to get there?

In A Perfect World

Write down, in detail, how you would like your life to look like in five years (marriage, education, career, self-improvement, etc.)

On the left, write the things that will help you get there. On the right, list what could hold you back from that dream.

NOTES

MAKING A NEW CHAIN

(Part Two)

...ONE LINK AT A TIME

SESSION THIRTEEN
Making A New Chain (Part Two)
Developing New Patterns

SESSION GOALS

- Examine the subject of change, how to truly attain it in areas of your life with God's help, and move forward in freedom, chained no more
- Reflect on the areas that need to be built up in the future and strategize about how you will make those changes

JUST FOR YOU

Change can be difficult, especially if we have had the same patterns and habits for a long time. It takes one step at a time and making strong efforts to change. It can be freeing and exciting when we finally realize we did it!

Some changes are easier to make than others, and some habits take longer to break than others, but the first step to change is identifying a goal of change. Then determine the steps and take those steps one at a time with strong resolve and purpose.

God wants you to be the best you can be and to accomplish all He has planned for you ... and so do we! There is *hope* for you and a better future. May God bless you as you go through this final chapter into your future.

Do not conform any longer to the patterns of this world, but be transformed by the renewing of your mind, Then you will be able to test and approve what God's will is—His good, pleasing and perfect will.
—Rom. 12:2

Change

The first step toward *change* is awareness.
The second step is *acceptance*.
The third step is *action*.

At the beginning of this class, on page 4, "Links of Issues," you checked the issues that you see in yourself. Take a look at page 4 to see how far you have come in healing! Awareness of these issues is the first step toward healing. We have addressed most of them throughout the past twelve weeks. Facing those issues, seeing where they began, and learning how God can heal them has hopefully led you toward a much healthier and brighter future.

My son, do not forget my teaching, but keep my commands in your heart, for they will prolong your life many years and bring you prosperity. Let love and faithfulness never leave you; bind them around your neck, write them on the tablet of your heart. Then you will win favor and a good name in the sight of God and man. Trust in the Lord with all your heart and lean not on your own understanding. In all your ways acknowledge Him and He will make your paths straight.
(Proverbs 3:1-6)

Steps to Change

KNOW THE INFORMATION—Become a student of God's Word, the Bible.

MEMORIZATION—It is important not to just read the Bible but also to make it part of your thinking by memorizing scripture.

MEDITATION—The process of working biblical truth over and over in the mind so you can gain deeper insight into its meaning.

IMAGINATION—Picture yourself living the changes you need to make and consider how you can be a different person.

APPLICATION—Make the change and purposely do it every single day. Say in strength, "I will *choose* to change."

"Change your mind and transform your life!"
—"A Mind Renewed by God" written by Dr. Kimball Hodge

Rebuilding Your Life

You have gone through many weeks of evaluating your life and exploring the effects that the divorce of your parents and other painful childhood experiences had on you as an adult. You have looked at God's love for you and how much He values you. You have hopefully learned about His forgiveness and His grace on a deeper level.

Now is the time to begin building new "links" toward a brighter and healthier future. Please indicate the following areas you want to rebuild in your life.

_____ My ability to trust people

_____ Being able to make a commitment and stick with it

_____ Not feeling as if I am on the outside looking in

_____ Not being so afraid of being rejected by others

_____ Learning how to control my anger

_____ Learning how to have a closer walk with Jesus Christ

_____ Being able to forgive someone and move on

_____ Building my confidence/understanding my worth

_____ Learning not to compare myself to others but to see my own value and theirs

_____ Learning not to let my emotions rule me or cloud my good judgment

Other areas _____

_____

_____

Rebuilding Your Life: Workpage

On the previous page, you checked the areas that you want to rebuild in your life. Now, please consider all of those areas, write out ways you are going to help make them happen and what you are willing to do to achieve them. Following that, write down the benefits you hope to see because of your efforts.

ISSUE #1 _____

WHAT YOU ARE GOING TO DO _____

_____

_____

_____

BENEFITS _____

_____

_____

ISSUE #2 _____

WHAT YOU ARE GOING TO DO _____

_____

_____

_____

BENEFITS _____

_____

_____

ISSUE #3 _____

WHAT YOU ARE GOING TO DO _____

_____

_____

BENEFITS _____

_____

_____

ISSUE #4 _____

WHAT YOU ARE GOING TO DO _____

_____

_____

BENEFITS _____

_____

_____

ISSUE #5 _____

WHAT YOU ARE GOING TO DO _____

_____

_____

BENEFITS _____

_____

_____

Links Learned

Please write some of the things you learned in *Chained No More*, and how you hope they will affect your life now. You may look back through this book to refresh your memory.

Putting Feet To Your Prayers

We can pray all day and wait for God to answer without doing our part and taking the necessary steps with His leading. Example: praying for a better job but not getting out there and interviewing. Or praying that God will give you an A on your exam, but not studying for it.

What are some prayer requests you have asked God about lately, and how have you done your part? List them below.

REQUEST:_____
_____

MY PART:_____
_____

REQUEST:_____
_____

MY PART:_____
_____

REQUEST:_____
_____

MY PART:_____
_____

REQUEST:_____
_____

MY PART:_____
_____

CONGRATULATIONS! YOU DID IT!

> We hope you have benefitted from *Chained No More*, and that God has done a mighty work in you over the last few months.
>
> We pray you can move forward in your faith, in strength, knowing that the Holy Spirit is there to guide you toward a much brighter and healthier future.
>
> *May God bless you with His joy!*

"Chained No More" Debrief Form

NAME _____ **AGE** _____

LOCATION OF CLASS _____ **CLASS DATES** _____

On a scale of 1-10, how helpful did you find *Chained No More*? _____

What was the most effective part? _____

Why? _____

_____

What was the least effective? _____

Why? _____

_____

On a scale of 1-10, please rate the following:

Class size (_____) _____

Class dynamic (_____) _____

Class leaders (_____) _____

Classroom (_____) _____

Adequate time to share (_____) _____

Effective and thought-provoking questions (_____) _____

Spiritual emphasis (_____) _____

Practical tools for future success in life (_____) _____

Effective healing and growth (_____) _____

Please comment and give suggestions below so we can continue to improve this program for effectiveness and success. Thank you for your input and for participating in *Chained No More*.

NOTE: Upon completing this form, please give it to your leader or send it to: Robyn B Ministries   P.O. Box 71726   Springfield, OR 97475

102

Chained No More

CREDITS AND RESOURCES

CONTRIBUTORS:

Elsa Colopy, speaker and author (www.elsakokcolopy.com)—Colorado Springs, Colorado

Pastor Colin Halstead, MA therapist, pastor of Renewal Ministries at First Baptist Church of Eugene—Eugene, Oregon (colinh@fbceugene.com)

Dr. Kimball Hodge III, D. Min. pastor and author—Central Point, Oregon

Linda Ranson-Jacobs, speaker, writer, and developer of *Divorce Care for Kids (hlp4.com)* —Navarre, Florida

Dr. Marlin Schultz, D.Min., marriage/family therapist—Eugene, Oregon

Krista Smith, Developer of *The Big D... Divorce Thru the Eyes of a Teen* —Big Lake, Minnesota (sonsetpointministries.com)

Many people interviewed are adult children of divorce, willing to share their stories and the many effects that their parents' divorce had on their lives.

Most importantly, the Lord God, His guidance in writing this material, and whose Word is the best contribution of all.

RESOURCE MATERIALS:

The Bible—God's Word

Between Two Worlds by Elizabeth Marquardt, Three Rivers Press, 2005

A Mind Renewed by God by Dr. Kimball Hodge III, Harvest House Publishers, 1998 (kimlyndahodge@gmail.com)

The Big D...Divorce Thru the Eyes of a Teen, by Krista Smith, AMFM Press, 2010 (sonsetpointministries.com)

Divorce Care for Kids by Linda Jacobs, Church Initiative, 2004 (hlp4.com)

Adult Children of Divorce by Jim Conway InterVarsity Press, 1990